Violent Dances Fade · CHOREAE VIOLENTAE DISSOLVVNTVR
Libertarian Poetical Fragments

SITIS PERPETVA

A Collection of fifty-one Latin Epigrams by
Stefano Losi

with English and Italian translations

MMXVII

Violent Dances Fade · CHOREAE VIOLENTAE DISSOLVVNTVR
Libertarian Poetical Fragments

A multimedia art and poetry project of
Stefano Losi

Familia mi · vobis
Catvlle · frater mi · tibi

New York – Milan – London
www.ViolentDancesFade.com
editor@violentdancesfade.com

ISBN: 978-0-578-18259-9

*"Timeless · On the contrary, inside time · And beyond
Significant · Blunt · Stirring, most of all"*

Marco MATHIEU
Writer and Journalist · La Repubblica, Rome

"This is a "splendid union" · Poetry as universal value"

Antonio Maria COSTA
Under-Secretary-General · United Nations

"Most impressive work · A scholarly writer"

Steve AOKI
Writer and Musician · Los Angeles

"Stefano seizes the gold that the moment presents"

Renato MIRACCO
Art Critic and Historian · Washington DC

"A very physical art · Raw material · And most importantly, alive"

Roberto FARANO
Composer and Musician · Turin

*"Stefano moves me with his words, forms and vision
almost as much as he inspires me with his thirst for life"*

Jonny HETHERINGTON
Composer and Musician · Vancouver

"Rich of sensuality and sensibility, the lines provide colour to the eyes"

Samira LEGLIB
Journalist · La Repubblica, New York

*"One of the rare artists who can negotiate seemingly opposing disciplines
with rigor, and unite them in one cathartic gesture"*

Chambliss GIOBBI
Artist, Actor and Composer · New York

Violent Dances Fade · CHOREAE VIOLENTAE DISSOLVVNTVR
Libertarian Poetical Fragments

*"QVOD DESIDERAS AVTEM MAGNVM
ET SVMMVM EST DEOQVE VICINVM · NON CONCVTI"*

L · A · SENECA

On the front cover: "CALIGINES" (detail)
Steel, White Onyx and LED Lights (17"x17"x2" · 43x43x5 cm)

Table of contents · Indice

"PLVS VNO MANEAT PERENNE SAECLO"

Indice

Violent Dances Fade · CHOREAE VIOLENTAE DISSOLVVNTVR
Libertarian Poetical Fragments

Table of contents

Violent Dances Fade · CHOREAE VIOLENTAE DISSOLVVNTVR
Libertarian Poetical Fragments

Biography · *Biografia*

PERTVRBATIONE ANIMI GIGNOR
NON INTERMISSO MOTV PONTI METHYMNAE

Biografia

Sono generato dall'inquietudine
Il movimento ininterrotto dei mari di Metimna

STEFANO LOSI è nato nel 1969 sul lago di Como, vicino a Milano, dove ha ricevuto un'educazione classica in letteratura ed arti visive. Dopo la laurea all'Università Luigi Bocconi di Milano del 1993, ha ricoperto posizioni manageriali in diverse istituzioni internazionali, ed è ora ufficiale senior dell'Organizzazione delle Nazioni Unite a New York, dove è anche Presidente del Circolo Culturale Letterario. Nel 2005 è stato nominato *Cavaliere della Repubblica Italiana* dal Presidente Ciampi.

"Violent Dances Fade · Choreae Violentae Dissolvvntvr" è il suo progetto di arti multimediali e poesia, creato a Milano nel 1991, e poi sviluppato a Londra e New York. "Choreae Violentae Dissolvvntvr" combina sculture in bronzo, acciaio, vetro e luci LED, musica contemporanea e spoken word, e studi su lino della figura umana in olii e minerali ossidati, con una poesia epigrammatica Latina. Dopo una lunga serie di eventi organizzati fino dai primi anni '90 in Europa, che hanno incluso mostre e letture di poesia in spazi sia formali che alternativi, da gallerie a unioni di lavoratori e centri sociali, la sua arte ha ricevuto l'onore di diverse mostre personali alle Nazioni Unite ed in affermate gallerie di New York. La sua poesia e' apparsa in antologie letterarie internazionali, quali Retina Literary Journal. Antonio Maria Costa, Sotto Segretario-Generale delle Nazioni Unite, ha scritto: *"È questo un connubio splendido. C'è nelle parole di queste poesie la stessa speranza che nutro quando osservo il mondo."*

Quattro volumi di arte e poesia sono stai pubblicati nel 1996, 2001, 2010 e 2013, fornendo una prospettiva del lavoro dell'autore nei rispettivi periodi creativi. L'arte di Stefano Losi è stata parte di diverse pubblicazioni internazionali, tra cui un volume su artisti contemporanei italiani curato da Renato Miracco, e pubblicato sotto gli auspici del Ministero degli Affari Esteri.
L'autore continua a creare arti visive e poesia a Chelsea, New York.

www.ViolentDancesFade.com
editor@violentdancesfade.com

Biography

I am generated by restlessness
The uninterrupted movement of the seas of Methymna

STEFANO LOSI was born in 1969 in Lake Como, near Milan, where he was classically educated in literature and fine arts. After his graduate degree at the Luigi Bocconi University of Milan in 1993, he covered senior management roles in different international institutions, and he is currently senior official of the United Nations in New York, where he is also President of the UNSRC Literary Cultural Circle. In 2005 he was nominated *Knight of the Italian Republic* by President Ciampi.

"Violent Dances Fade · Choreae Violentae Dissolvvntvr" is his multimedia art and poetry project created in Milan in 1991, and further developed in London and New York. It combines sculptures in bronze, steel, cast glass and LED lights, contemporary music and spoken word, and linen studies of the human figure in oils and oxidized metal minerals, with an epigrammatic Latin poetry. After a long series of events organized since the early 1990s in Europe, including shows and poetry readings in formal and alternative spaces, ranging from galleries, to workers unions and social centers, his art has been honored with different solo exhibitions at the United Nations and in established galleries in New York. His poetry has been part of international literary antologies, as Retina Literary Journal. Antonio Maria Costa, Under-Secretary-General of the United Nations, wrote: *"This is a splendid union. In the words of these poems I find the same hope I cherish when I observe the world."*

Four books collecting his art and epigrams, providing an overview of the author's work in the respective creative periods, were published in 1996, 2001, 2010 and 2013. Stefano Losi's work has been featured in different international publications, among which a book on Italian contemporary artists curated by Renato Miracco, and published under the auspices of the Italian Ministry of Foreign Affairs.

The author continues to create art and poetry in Chelsea, New York.

www.ViolentDancesFade.com
editor@violentdancesfade.com

Violent Dances Fade · CHOREAE VIOLENTAE DISSOLVVNTVR
Libertarian Poetical Fragments

Preface · Prefazione

INQVIETVDO · PVRA RATIO · SITIS PERPETVA

Prefazione

Inquietudine · Ragione pura · Sete continua

Preface

Unquietness · Pure reason · Continuous thirst

Elegies and Epigrams · Epigrammi ed Elegie

Violent Dances Fade · CHOREAE VIOLENTAE DISSOLVVNTVR
Libertarian Poetical Fragments

RESPIRO

I breathe

Purple flower
In my hand

Touch me
With lips moist of dew
Sprinkle me with kisses

Sensation of imminent rain
Outlines a pause
In the sigh of existence

Free
Devoid of any decadence
Intangible to time

As an imperfect lover

I breathe

I breathe

RESPIRO

PVRPVREVS FLOS
IN MEA MANV

ME LEVITER ATTINGE
VMIDIS EX RORE LABRIS
ME BASIIS IRRORA

IMMINENTIS SENSVS IMBRIS
MORAM
IN SVSPIRIO ESSE DELINEAT

LIBER
OMNI CORRVPTIONE PRIVATVS
TEMPORE INVIOLABILIS

IMPERFECTVS AMANS

RESPIRO

RESPIRO

RESPIRO (detail)
Bronze and Cast Glass (16"x12"x12" · 40x30x30cm)

RESPIRO (detail)
Bronze and Cast Glass (16"x12"x12" · 40x30x30cm)

Respiro

Purpureo fiore
Nella mia mano

Sfiorami
Con labbra umide di rugiada
Irrorami di baci

Sensazione di pioggia imminente
Delinea una pausa
Nel sospiro dell'essere

Libero
Privo di alcuna decadenza
Intangibile al tempo

Quale imperfetto amante

Respiro

Respiro

PALVS

Lagoon

Intermediate landscape
Scraped in dull ash of features
By dampness

Hides
The stare dressing its paleness

Impalpable objects I touch

Nothing from being
Admits belonging

I am so impure

Lagoon

PALVS

MEDIA REGIO
VLIGINE LINEAMENTORVM
NON PERLVCIDO EX CINERE INCISA

ASPECTVM QVI VESTIAT EIVS PALLOREM
DISSIMVLAT

LEVITER RES TENVISSIMAS ATTINGO

NIHIL
ESSE PERTINET

ADEO IMPVRVS SVM

PALVS

Laguna

Paesaggio intermedio
Scalfito in opaca cenere di lineamenti
Da umidità

Nasconde
Lo sguardo che ne vesta il pallore

Oggetti impalpabili sfioro

Niente dall'essere
Concede appartenenza

Sono in tal modo impuro

Laguna

IMBER

The rain
Follows the beat
Of your rhythmic dance

Raises the scent of the soil moved
By your graceful feet

Most fresh water
Soaks your hair
Then flows along their lines
Framing your trembling visage
Your black eyes
The gentle nose
Your thin lips

Flows down along your body
Caresses your small breast
The smooth arms
Your nude back

Takes possession of your light clothes

At last I venture to bring near
My palm
With insecure hands

Still shaken
I can not tell you what I feel

Listen

The rain
Is already doing it for me

Rain

IMBER
MODVLATAE SALTATIONIS TVAE
PVLSVM PROSEQVITVR

A SVAVIBVS PEDIBVS TVIS
MOTAE TERRAE ODOREM TOLLIT

AQVA VIRENTISSIMA
CAPILLVM TVVM MADIDAT
POSTEA FLVIT SECVNDVM EIVS LINEAS
AD CIRCVMDANDVM TREMENTEM VVLTVM TVVM
TVOS OCVLOS ATROS
DVLCEM NASVM
SICCA TVA LABRA

DEINDE SECVNDVM CORPVS TVVM DESCENDIT
PERMVLCET PARVVM SINVM
EXPOLITOS LACERTOS
DORSVM TVVM NVDVM

VESTEM TVAM LEVEM ASSVMIT

TANDEM
ME AD PALMAM MEAM ADMOVENDVM IMPELLO
INCERTIS MANIBVS

ADHVC COMMOTVS
TE QVOD SENTIO DICERE NON POSSVM

AVSCVLTA

IMBER
PER ME ID IAM FACIT

IMBER

La pioggia
Segue il battito
Della tua danza ritmata

Alza l'odore della terra mossa
Dai tuoi piedi aggraziati

Acqua freschissima
Madida i tuoi capelli
Poi scorre lungo le loro linee
Ad incorniciare il tuo volto tremante
I tuoi occhi neri
Il naso dolce
Le tue labbra sottili

Scende lungo il tuo corpo
Accarezza il tuo seno piccolo
Le braccia levigate
La tua schiena nuda

Fa proprie le tue vesti leggere

Finalmente mi spingo ad avvicinare
Il mio palmo
Con mani insicure

Ancora scosso
Non posso dirti quello che sento

Ascolta

La pioggia
Lo sta già facendo per me

Pioggia

ARSVRIS SVB MVRIS

Under the burnt walls
The sand remains

Purified

I recite the monologue
Of the essence and of the continuous relapse
Of mortal love

Tears and words
The art of power

Quiet as only a god
Can be

Under the burnt walls

ARSVRIS SVB MVRIS
ARENA QVIESCIT

PVRIFICATA

RECITO
INTIMVM SERMONEM
VIS ATQVE PERPETVI INTERITVS AMORIS MORTALIS

LACRIMAE VERBAQVE
ARS POTESTATIS

QVIETVS TAMQVAM SOLVS DEVS
ESSE POTEST

ARSVRIS SVB MVRIS

Sotto le mura arse
La sabbia rimane

Purificata

Recito il monologo
Dell'essenza e della ricaduta continua
Dell'amore mortale

Lacrime e parole
L'arte del potere

Quieto come solo un dio
Può essere

Sotto le mura

TE SENTIO

As you appear in the garden
We glance at each other

Then you expose yourself
As nobody has ever seen
Innocent as a vestal

Most beautiful solitary flower
Caressed by the wind
Nourished by the sun and the morning rime

I feel you
My fingers on your mouth
Hesitant

Your lips moist of dew
Drops go along your gentle skin
Your breast
Sweetest and pale

I dare to run away
While you laugh adorably

The dew of your lips remains on mine
I taste its flavour
Perfumed erotic trembling

I feel you

TE IN HORTO APPARENTE
OCVLOS PERMVTAMVS

TE DEINDE IN CONSPECTV EXPONIS
MODO NEMO VNQVAM VIDIT
INNOCENS TAMQVAM VESTALIS

PVLCHERRIMVS SOLVS FLOS
VENTO PERMVLSVS
SOLE ET MATVTINI TEMPORIS PRVINIS NVTRITVS

TE SENTIO
DIGITI MEI SVPER TVVM OS
HAESITANTES

LABRA TVA VMIDA RORE
STILLAE MOLLEM CVTEM TVAM PERCVRRVNT
PECTVS TVVM
DVLCISSIMVM ET PALLIDVM

FVGERE AVDEO
DVM AMABILITER RIDES

LABRORVM ROS TVORVM SVPER MEA MANET
SAPOREM SVVM GVSTO
FRAGRANTEM AMATORIVM TREMOREM

TE SENTIO

Al tuo apparire in giardino
Scambiamo sguardi

Poi tu ti esponi
Come nessuno ha mai visto
Innocente come una vestale

Bellissimo fiore solitario
Accarezzato dal vento
Nutrito dal sole e dalla brina del mattino

Ti sento
Le mie dita sulla tua bocca
Insicure

Le tue labbra umide di rugiada
Gocce percorrono la tua pelle morbida
Il tuo seno
Dolcissimo e pallido

Oso fuggire
Mentre tu ridi amabilmente

La rugiada delle tue labbra è rimasta sulle mie
Ne gusto il sapore
Profumato tremore erotico

Ti sento

TIBIARVM TREMOR

Beyond the sea
I search for the one I knew

You
Are waiting for me
As unwanted breath

When I see you
You are dancing
You follow the rhythm of the delicate fingers
That beat the pale and unquiet skin
Of the drums of Lesbos
Dark melodies resound

Then you look at me
Still breathless
I recognize traces of tears in your eyes
Crying you pretend to curse me
I feel a tremble
Of flutes
And the horizons
Reflect your glance

I would like you spoke to me
Pretending to be my lover

I would like you set free
The soul you seduced me

Tremble of flutes

VLTRA MARE
QVAERO EAM QVAM COGNOSCEBAM

TV
ME EXSPECTAS
QVASI NON CVPITVS SPIRITVS

CVM TE VIDEO
SALTAS
MOVES AD LEVIVM DIGITORVM NVMERVM
PERCVTIENTIVM PALLIDVM INQVIETVMQVE CORIVM
TYMPANORVM LESBI
GRAVES MODI RESONANT

POSTEA ME INTVERIS
ADHVC ANHELANS
ANIMADVERTO SIGNA LACRIMORVM IN OCVLIS TVIS
FLENS ME EXSECRARI SIMVLAS
SENTIO TREMOREM
TIBIARVM
ET VLTIMAE CAELI PARTES
ASPECTVM TVVM REPERCVTIVNT

VELLEM CVM ME LOQVERERIS
SIMVLARES AMANS MEA ESSE

VELLEM LIBERARES
ANIMAM ADLEXISTI

TIBIARVM TREMOR

Oltre il mare
Cerco colei che conoscevo

Tu
Mi stai aspettando
Come respiro non voluto

Quando ti vedo
Stai danzando
Segui il ritmo delle dita lievi
Che battono la pelle pallida ed inquieta
Dei tamburi di Lesbo
Risuonano cupi melodie

Poi mi guardi
Ancora ansimante
Mi accorgo di tracce di lacrime nei tuoi occhi
In pianto fingi di maledirmi
Avverto un tremito
Di flauti
E gli orizzonti
Riflettono il tuo sguardo

Vorrei che tu mi parlassi
Che fingessi di essere la mia amante

Vorrei che liberassi
L'anima che mi hai sedotto

Tremito di flauti

OBITVS

I was born from eastern seas
From unquietness

Adopted by peoples
Without name

I feel the paleness
Slowly taking possession of my body

Finally free

I caress
The oxidised walls of Mycenae
I see the symbols of eternal decline
I taste their amber wine

I am yours

Obitvs

NATVS EX ORIENTIS MARIBVS SVM
EX TREPIDATIONE

ADOPTATVS A GENTIBVS
SINE NOMINE

SENTIO PALLOREM
SENSIM CORPORE MEO POTIRI

TANDEM LIBER

ROBIGINE OBDVCTA MOENIA MYCENARVM
MANV PERMVLCEO
VIDEO IMAGINES AETERNI OCCASVS
EORVM ELECTRO MERVM GVSTO

TVVS SVM

OBITVS

Sono nato da mari orientali
Dall'inquietudine

Adottato da popoli
Senza nome

Sento il pallore
Lentamente impossessarsi del mio corpo

Finalmente libero

Accarezzo
Le mura ossidate di Micene
Vedo i simboli dell'eterno declino
Ne gusto il vino ambrato

Sono tuo

Obitvs

TÆDIVM

Autumn
A distant twilight

With eyes looking inward
I sit in silence
To observe the decomposition of the body

Malaise
Mute presence

Behind a veil of melancholy
Encircled by light
Exhales poetry

Malaise

AVTVMNVS
LONGINQVVM CREPVSCVLVM

VERSIS IN ANIMO OCVLIS
TACITE SEDEO
AD DISSOLVTIONEM COPORIS OBSERVANDAM

TAEDIVM
MVTA PRAESENTIA

POST EX AEGRITVDINE ANIMI VELVM
LVCE CIRCVMFVSVM
EXHALAT POESIN

TAEDIVM

Autunno
Un lontano crepuscolo

Con lo sguardo rivolto dentro
Mi siedo in silenzio
Ad osservare la decomposizione del corpo

Malessere
Muta presenza

Dietro un velo di malinconia
Circonfuso di luce
Esala poesia

Malessere

CONGRVENTIAE

I write verses

Told
By the ripe ears
Of wheat
Stirred by the warm wind
Of noon

Stolen
By craters of wine
Fragrant of resins
Dampened by the dew
Of the evening

I search for consolation in the poetry

Irresistible attraction
Of subtle correspondences

Correspondences

SCRIBO VERSVS

NARRATOS
MATVRIS ARISTIS
FRVMENTI
VENTO CALIDO MERIDIEI
AGITATI

ABLATOS
DE CRATERIBVS MERI
RESINARVM FRAGRANTIBVS
VESPERI RORE
MADIDIS

ME POESE CONSOLOR

DVLCEDINE VEHEMENTI
SVBTILIVM CONGRVENTIARVM

CONGRVENTIAE

Scrivo versi

Raccontati
Dalle spighe mature
Di grano
Mosso dal vento caldo
Del meriggio

Rubati
Da crateri di vino
Profumati di resine
Bagnati dalla rugiada
Della sera

Cerco conforto nella poesia

Attrazione irresistibile
Di corrispondenze sottili

Corrispondenze

IMBER ARIDVS

I am generated by restlessness
The uninterrupted movement of the seas of Methymna

Tormented
By a continuous thirst
Powered by a rain of ash and copper

The insistent caress
Of a most terse sand
Projects
In opaque light
My features of burned soil
The thin hands smoothed by the sun

Amongst the wind
Virginal trembling
I approach my lips to yours
Livid
Wet of salt

Slowly
You bring to you my body
Now stripped of shadow

Finally free

As a god
After death
I sit behind your eyes of ash

Arid rain

PERTVRBATIONE ANIMI GIGNOR
NON INTERMISSO MOTV PONTI METHYMNAE

SITI CONTINVA
TORTVS
IMBRE EX CINERE ET AERE ALITA

ASSIDVAE BLANDITIAE
AREANAE PVRISSIMAE
IN NON PERLVCIDAM LVCEM
ARSIS EX TERRIS LINEAMENTA MEA
MITTVNT
MANVS SVBTILES SOLE EXPOLITAS

IN VENTO
VIRGINALI TREMORE
LABRA MEA TVIS ADMOVEO
LIVIDIS
EX SALI VDIS

SENSIM
AD TE CORPVS MEVM DVCIS
IAM VMBRA NVDVM

AD VLTIMVM LIBER

POSTEA MORTEM
TAMQVAM DEVS
SEDEO PONE TVOS EX CINERE OCVLOS

IMBER ARIDVS

Sono generato dall'inquietudine
Il movimento ininterrotto dei mari di Metimna

Tormentato
Da una sete continua
Alimentata da una pioggia di cenere e rame

La carezza insistente
Di una sabbia tersissima
Proietta
In luce opaca
I miei lineamenti di terre bruciate
Le mani sottili levigate dal sole

Fra il vento
Tremito verginale
Accosto le mie labbra alle tue
Livide
Umide di sale

Lentamente
Porti a te il mio corpo
Ormai spoglio d'ombra

Finalmente libero

Come un dio
Dopo la morte
Siedo dietro i tuoi occhi di cenere

Pioggia arida

FORMAE MVTATIO

A summer morning
We return from the garden of hyacinths
Of violet and purple

Of the intact scent

Thin leaves
Caress
Your ankles
Elegant and pale

Damp of fresh dew

Your breath on my skin
Makes me feel so inadequate
Impure

Metamorphosis
Of the ritual of innocence

Metamorphosis

AESTATE MANE
A HORTIS VIOLACEIS PVRPVREISQVE
HYACINTHORVM REDIMVS

ODORE INCORRVPTO

SVBTILIA FOLIA
ELEGANTES ATQVE PALLIDOS
TALOS TVOS
PERMVLCENT

FRIGIDO RORE VDOS

SPIRITVS TVVS IN MEAM CVTIM
EFFECIT VT INDIGNITATEM IMPVDICITIAMQVE MEAM
SENTIAM

FORMAE MVTATIO
CASTITATIS RITVS

FORMAE MVTATIO

Un mattino d'estate
Torniamo dai giardini dei giacinti
Di viola e porpora

Dal profumo intatto

Le foglie sottili
Accarezzano
Le tue caviglie
Eleganti e pallide

Umide di rugiada fresca

Il tuo respiro sulla mia pelle
Mi fa sentire talmente inadeguato
Impuro

Metamorfosi
Del rito dell'innocenza

Metamorfosi

VMBRAE CVPRESSORVM

A slow kiss
Amongst the evening verses

Shadows of cypresses
Collect the western winds

A primordial rain
Naked
Soaks the soil
Parched with scent of amber

Lies buried
My loved sense
Of poetry

Shadows of cypresses

LENTVM BASIVM
VESPERIS INTER VERSVS

VMBRAE CVPRESSORVM
OCCIDENTIS VENTVM COLLIGVNT

PRIMVS IMBER
NVDVS
TERRAM IMBVIT
ELECTRI ODORIS SITIENTEM

IACET
AMATVS SENSVS MEVS
POESIS

VMBRAE CVPRESSORVM

Un bacio lento
Fra i versi della sera

Ombre di cipressi
Raccolgono il vento di ponente

Una primordiale pioggia
Ignuda
Madida la terra
Assetata di odore d'ambra

Giace sepolto
Il mio amato senso
Di poesia

Ombre di cipressi

CARMEN FVNEBRE

In the evening veil
Beyond the desperate blue cypresses
Reclined by the faint breeze

A pale glimmer
Reflects
On the lake of darkest emerald
Almost motionless

Interrupting the silence
A flute laments
Vain tears

Soaked with crying
Your hands
Gently close my afflicted eyelid

They accompany me
In the peace of sleep

Whilst fragile waves
Rhythmically caress
The white sand
Dressed of innocence

Uninterrupted

Funerary lyric

IN CALIGINE VESPERI
PRAETER CAERVLEAS CVPRESSVS OMNI SPE DEIECTAS
LENI AVRA RECLINATAS

LANGVIDVM LVMEN
IMAGINEM SVAM IN PREFVSCO LACV SMARAGDO
CONTEMPLATVR
QVASI IMMOTO

INTERRVPTO SILENTIO
TIBIAE VANAS LACRIMAS
QVERVNTVR

FLETV IMBVTAE
MANVS TVAE
LEVITER PALPEBRAS MEAS GRAVES ADTINGVNT

IN PACEM SOMNI
ME COMITANTVR

DVM FRAGILES VNDAE
IN NVMERVM PERMVLCENT
PVRAM ARENAM
CASTITATE VESTITAM

NON INTERMISSAE

CARMEN FVNEBRE

Nel velo della sera
Oltre i disperati cipressi blu
Reclinati dalla brezza lieve

Un chiarore pallido
Si specchia
Sul lago di smeraldo scurissimo
Quasi immoto

Interrompendo il silenzio
Un flauto lamenta
Lacrime futili

Intrise di pianto
Le tue mani
Sfiorano la mia palpebra dolorosa

Mi accompagnano
Nella pace del sonno

Mentre onde fragili
Accarezzano ritmicamente
La tersa arena
Vestita di innocenza

Ininterrotte

Canto funebre

MYRTORVM HORTVS

I sit with you
At the side of the garden of myrtles

Still unviolated

I observe
The gentle dew
That wraps in the morning
The solitary flowers of Pimpleia

Two drops run after each other
Then fall in the fine soil

The instant of contemplation
Fixes in me the musicality of your verse

Hidden sense
Of the becoming of being

Garden of myrtles

TECVM ADSIDO
MYRTORVM IN HORTI MARGINIBVS

ADHVC INVIOLATI

VENVSTVM ROREM
MANE VELANTEM
SOLOS FLORES PIMPLEOS
INTVEOR

DVAE INSEQVVNTVR GVTTAE
POSTEA IN SVBTILEM TERRAM DECIDVNT

TEMPORIS MOMENTVM CONTEMPLATIONIS
IN ME SVAVITATEM VERSVM TVVM FIRMAT

ABDITVM SENSVM
VITAE IN FIERI

MYRTORVM HORTVS

Mi siedo con te
Ai margini del giardino di mirti

Ancora inviolato

Osservo
La rugiada gentile
Che al mattino avvolge
I solitari fiori di Pimpleia

Due gocce si rincorrono
Poi cadono nella terra fine

L'istante della contemplazione
Fissa in me la musicalità del tuo verso

Senso nascosto
Del divenire dell'essere

Giardino di mirti

MORS LACRIMIS PERFVSA

It rains

Tearful death

Water
Sweet and lucent
Flows unquiet

Along your hair of violet
The face pale of silver
The thin blue hands

Under the rain
I kiss your gelid lips

Slowly
You conduct to you my body
Now shadeless

Whilst it continues to rain

Tearful death

PLVIT

MORS LACRIMIS PERFVSA

AQVA
NITENS ET SVAVIS
FLVIT INQVIETA

SECVNDVM VIOLA CAPILLVM TVVM
PALLIDVM ARGENTO VVLTVM
TENVES CAERVLEAS MANVS

SVB IMBRE
GELIDA LABRA TVA BASIO

LENTE
AD TE CORPVS MEVM DVCIS
IAM SINE VMBRA

DVM PLVERE PERGIT

MORS LACRIMIS PERFVSA

Piove

Morte lacrimosa

Acqua
Dolce e lucente
Scorre Inquieta

Lungo i tuoi capelli di viola
Il viso pallido di argento
Le sottili mani blu

Sotto la pioggia
Bacio le tue labbra gelide

Lentamente
conduci a te il mio corpo
Ormai senza ombra

Mentre continua a piovere

Morte lacrimosa

AMARA TERRA

You forgot me

My mute shadow wanders amongst the flowers of lotus
Flatters on the stagnant water

Whilst on a bed white of ivory
My remains rest quiet

From my pyre evaporates a myrrh of darkest honey

As my ashes
In an unreal light
Return to the bitter soil

Bitter soil

OBLITA MEI ES

MVTA VMBRA MEA LOTI INTER FLORES VAGATVR
SVPRA STAGNANTEM AQVAM VOLITAT

DVM IN EBVRNEO LECTO
MEMBRA MEA REQVIESCVNT

MYRRHA OBSCVRISSIMO MELLE A PYRA MEA EXHALAT

TVM CINIS MEVS
IN COMMENTICIA LVCE
AMARAM IN TERRAM REDIT

AMARA TERRA

Mi hai dimenticato

La mia ombra muta vaga fra i fiori di loto
Aleggia sull'acqua stagnante

Mentre su un letto bianco d'avorio
Le mie membra riposano quiete

Dalla mia pira evapora una mirra di miele scurissimo

Quando le mie ceneri
In una luce irreale
Tornano nell'amara terra

Amara terra

BOMBYX BYZANTII

I have listened to your soft step
Your rhythmic breathing
In the dance

I have followed your hand sliding through your hair
Of amber silk of Byzantium

I want to taste
Your beauty
Pure

I want to keep
Your tears
In the palm of my hand

Sweetest token
Of your mortal love

Silk of Byzantium

LEVEM GRADVM TVVM AVSCVLTAVI
TVVM SPIRITVM MODVLATVM
IN CHOREA

MANVM TVAM FLVERE INTER CAPILLVM
EX SVCINA BOMBYCE BYZANTII SECVTVS SVM

VENVSTATEM TVAM
PVRAM
GVSTARE CVPIO

LACRIMAS TVAS
IN MANVS MEAE PALMA
CVPIO SERVARE

PIGNVS DVLCISSIMVM
AMORIS TVI MORTALIS

BOMBYX BYZANTII

Ho ascoltato il tuo passo lieve
Il tuo respiro ritmato
Nella danza

Ho seguito la tua mano scorrere fra i capelli
Di seta ambrata di Bisanzio

Voglio assaporare
La tua bellezza
Pura

Voglio conservare
Le tue lacrime
Nel palmo della mia mano

Pegno dolcissimo
Del tuo amore mortale

Seta di Bisanzio

EVANESCENS VESTALIS

Set the moon
You come back to life

Given up purity finally you come close

Whilst I try to steal a kiss from your thin mouth
Another time you escape
Evanescent vestal

With thin fingers you gently stop my lips
And run away laughing

Come back I beg you
Most lovable virgin

You know where to find me tonight

Evanescent vestal

LVNA OCCASA
AD VITAM REDIS

INTEGRITATE DONATA TANDEM ADPROPINQVAS

DVM FVRARI BASIVM ORI TVO SVBTILI EXPERIOR
TE RVRSVS ERIPIS
EVANESCENS VESTALIS

TERETIBVS DIGITIS DELICATE LABRA MEA MORARIS
ET RIDENS FVGIS

REDI TE ORO
VIRGO AMABILISSIMA

VBI ME HAC NOCTE INVENIRE SCIS

EVANESCENS VESTALIS

Tramontata la luna
Torni a vivere

Donata la purezza finalmente ti avvicini

Mentre tento di rubare un bacio alla tua bocca sottile
Ancora una volta ti sottrai
Evanescente vestale

Con dita affusolate delicatamente fermi le mie labbra
E fuggi ridente

Ti prego torna
Vergine amabilissima

Sai dove trovarmi questa notte

Evanescente vestale

DVLCISSIMVS POETA

I feel emptiness inside
Stronger than reason itself
My god

It still hurts
It pushes me deeper and deeper

I am so tired
I close my eyes
I look for some rest in the shadeless embrace of Hypnos

My brother
Let me come and visit you

My sweetest poet
Let me join you
In the evening dew

Sweetest poet

SOLITVDINEM IN ANIMO SENTIO
FORTIOREM QVAM RATIONEM IPSAM
DEE MI

ADHVC MIHI DOLOREM ADFERT
ME DEFERT MAGIS MAGISQVE

TAM FATIGATVS SVM
OCVLOS CLAVDO
SOMNI IN AMPLEXV SINE VMBRA QVIESCO

FRATER MI
TE VISERE MIHI PERMITTE

DVLCISSIME POETA MI
EFFICE VT MIHI LICEAT TE CONSEQVI
IN RORE VESPERTINO

DVLCISSIMVS POETA

Sento un vuoto dentro
Più forte della ragione stessa
Mio dio

Fa ancora male
Mi spinge sempre più in basso

Sono talmente stanco
Chiudo gli occhi
Cerco riposo nell'abbraccio senza ombre di Ipno

Fratello mio
Lasciami venire a trovarti

Mio dolcissimo poeta
Fa che possa raggiungerti
Nella rugiada della sera

Dolcissimo poeta

SITIS PERPETVA

Remembrance and Desire · Passion and Word

Endless thirst
To close the circle of hate

Endless thirst

MEMORIA DESIDERIVMQVE MOTVS ANIMI ET VERBVM

SITIS PERPETVA
VT FINEM CIRCVLO ODII FACIAT

SITIS PERPETVA

Ricordo e Desiderio · Passione e Parola

Sete continua
Per chiudere il cerchio dell'odio

Sete continua

CARDVVS

Amongst the ruins
I observe
A thistle of purple and thorns

Generated by the sorrows of the earth

Born from the dew of the Ethiopian desert

Amongst parched fields

Cracked
By the oxidised winds of the south

Its dart
Reflects
The essence of my words

The thistle

IN RVDERIBVS
CARDVVM PVRPVREVM ET SPINIS
INTVEOR

DOLORE TERRAE GENITVM

SOLITVDINIS AETHIOPICAE RORE PROCREATVM

IN ARIDIS AGRIS

MERIDIANIS OXYDO VENTIS
LACERATIS

ACVLEVS
VERBORVM VIM MEORVM
REPERCVTIT

CARDVVS

Tra le rovine
Osservo
Un cardo di porpora e spine

Generato dal dolore della terra

Nato dalla rugiada del deserto etiope

Fra campi riarsi

Screpolati
Dai venti ossidati del sud

Il suo strale
Riflette
L'essenza delle mie parole

Il cardo

QVASI POLLINEM

A child
Never conceived
Sits at the spring of illusions

Water gushes out
Constructed by romantic ideas

Impassible of infinity
She gathers the tale of the soul

Coagulated the violence
She takes on the sweetness of emotions
Nearly pollen

And transfigures the reason

My nostalgia of love
Protects her

Nearly pollen

PVELLVLA
NVMQVAM CONCEPTA
FALSARVM IMAGINVM FONTI ADSIDET

AQVA EFFLVIT
SVAVIBVS EX NOTIONIBVS CONSTRVCTA

EX INFINITO IMPERTVRBATA
ANIMAE NARRATIONEM COLLIGIT

VI COAGVLATA
ANIMI MOTVVM DVLCEDINEM SVMIT
QVASI POLLINEM

AC RATIONEM MVTAT

DESIDERIVM AMORIS MEVM
EAM PROTEGIT

QVASI POLLINEM

Una bambina
Mai concepita
Siede alla fonte delle illusioni

Sgorga acqua
Costruita da idee romantiche

Impassibile di infinito
Raccoglie il racconto dell'anima

Rappresa la violenza
Assume la dolcezza di emozioni
Quasi polline

E trasfigura la ragione

La mia nostalgia di amore
La protegge

Quasi polline

IN ELEGIA

I am
Rain · Sorrow · Rage

I sail
In the ocean of anguish
Primordial infinite
Of imperfect moments

Corrupted

Still rain
A continuous suffering
Then rage and sorrow

Lost
The individuality of emotions
In elegy
Reason unravels

In elegy

SVM
IMBER · DOLOR · IRA

ANGORIS IN MARI
NAVIGO
PRIMA INFINITATE
IMPERFECTORVM TEMPORIS MOMENTORVM

CORRVPTORVM

ITERVM IMBER
ADSIDVVM TAEDIVM
POSTEA IRA ATQVE DOLOR

PERDITIS
SINGVLI ANIMI MOTIBVS
IN ELEGIA
RATIO EXPLICAT

IN ELEGIA

Io sono
Pioggia · Sofferenza · Rabbia

Navigo
Nell'oceano dell'angoscia
Infinito primordiale
Di attimi imperfetti

Corrotti

Ancora pioggia
Un malessere continuo
Poi rabbia e sofferenza

Persa
L'individualità delle emozioni
In elegia
La ragione si dipana

In elegia

CALIGINES

Uncertain steps
In the dawning of haze

I feel the thoughts filtering through the walls

Then I stretch out the wings
In the cold mist

I am in the rain
Unsustainable

The dew

The origin

The frail light
That kisses
The mist of the morning

Haze

INCERTA GRADVS
INTER CALIGINES ILLVCESCENTES

COGITATIONES EX MVRIS FLVERE SENTIO

POSTEA ALAS EXTENDO
IN FRIGIDA NEBVLA

SVM IN IMBRE
INTOLERABILI

ROS

ORIGO

TENVIS LVX
BASIANS
CALIGINEM MANE

CALIGINES

CALIGINES (detail)
Steel, White Onyx and LED Lights (17"x17"x2" · 43x43x5cm)

CALIGINES (detail)
Steel, White Onyx and LED Lights (17"x17"x2" · 43x43x5cm)

Passi incerti
Nell'albeggiare di brume

Sento i pensieri filtrare dalle mura

Poi stendo le ali
Nella nebbia fredda

Sono nella pioggia
Insostenibile

La rugiada

L'origine

La tenue luce
Che bacia
La foschia del mattino

Brume

IRA

I exist since the beginning of time
Before the matter

I am the ire
In transformation

The destroyer god
The idol of false

I flatter
Over seas of salt
Ravaged by a primordial violence

Tongues of fire bring an intense rain
That beats the ruins of Megiddo

In an eternal twilight

Ire

SVM AB AETERNO
ANTE MATERIAM

SVM IRA
IN FIERI

EVERSOR DEVS
FICTI DEI SIMVLACRVM

VOLITO
SVPRA EX SALE MARIA
PRIMA VI DEVASTATA

IGNES VEHEMENTEM IMBREM FERVNT
QVI RVDERA MAGEDDI PERCVTIT

IN AETERNO OCCASV

IRA

Esisto da sempre
Da prima della materia

Sono l'ira
In trasformazione

Il dio distruttore
L'idolo del falso

Aleggio
Su mari di sale
Devastati da una violenza primordiale

Lingue di fuoco portano una pioggia intensa
Che percuote le rovine di Megiddo

In un tramonto eterno

Ira

ADHVC RESPIRO

Use me I pray you
My virgin
I want to taste the honey of your tormented kiss

Lead to you my body

Hate me
I pray you
Lacerate me

Hold my hand
Trembling of the blood of Hymenaeus
The cut flower
In which life is born and regenerates

You see I still can breathe

I still breathe

TE ME VTERE ORO
MEA VIRGO
DEGVSTARE MEL EXCRVCIATI BASII TVI VOLO

AD TE CORPVS MEVM DVCE

ODIVM IN ME HABE
TE ORO
LACERA ME

TENE MANVM MEAM
SANGVINE HYMENAEI TREMENTEM
RECISI FLORIS
IN QVO VITA NASCITVR ET RESTITVITVR

VIDES ADHVC RESPIRO

ADHVC RESPIRO

Ti prego usami
Vergine mia
Voglio gustare il miele del tuo bacio tormentato

Conduci a te il mio corpo

Odiami
Ti prego
Lacerami

Tieni la mia mano
Tremante del sangue di Imene
Il fiore reciso
In cui la vita nasce e si rigenera

Vedi riesco ancora a respirare

Ancora respiro

ARENAE LIBYCAE

Kiss me

On the Libyan sands
Amongst the rows of silphium of Cyrene

Bite my lips
Moist with dew

Whilst the sea is caressed
By the delicate fingers of the moon

From the earth raise
Fragrances of citrus trees
And bitter oranges

You are mine

Libyan sands

BASIA ME

IN ARENIS LIBYCIS
INTER ORDINES SILPHII CYRENES

MORDE LABRA MEA
EX RORE VDA

DVM AEQVOR
EXILIBVS LVNAE DIGITIS PERMVLCETVR

ACRIVM POMORVM ODORES
AVREORVM AMARORVMQVE MALORVM
A TERRA SVRGVNT

MEA ES

ARENAE LIBYCAE

Baciami

Sulle sabbie libiche
Fra i filari di silfio di Cirene

Mordimi le labbra
Umide di rugiada

Mentre il mare viene carezzato
Dalle dita tenui della luna

Dalla terra si alzano
Profumi di agrumi
E di arance amare

Sei mia

Sabbie libiche

RECORDATIO

With eyes of tears
I approach your tomb
Silent

Over the hill
Amongst the pale olive trees

A light breeze
Brings melodies of flutes
Distant

I bend on the ground
Soaked in tears

I hide in your embrace
Where troubles subside

And slowly I feel fainting

Whilst remembrance
Fragile reflection
Another time prevails

Remembrance

LACRIMANTIBVS CVM OCVLIS
SEPVLCRO TVO ADPROPINQVO
TACITO

IN COLLE
PALLIDIS IN OLEIS

LENIS AVRA
CANTVS TIBIARVM FERT
LONGINQVOS

ME IN TERRAM INCLINO
LACRIMIS MADIDAM

ME IN AMPLEXV TVO ABDO
VBI AERVMNAE CONSIDVNT

ET LENITER SENTIO ME ANIMO RELINQVI

DVM RECORDATIO
FRAGILIS REPERCVSSVS
ITERVM VINCIT

RECORDATIO

Con occhi di lacrime
Mi avvicino alla tua tomba
Silenziosa

Sulla collina
Fra i pallidi ulivi

Una brezza lieve
Porta melodie di flauti
Lontane

Mi chino sulla terra
Madida di pianto

Mi nascondo nel tuo abbraccio
Dove si placa l'affanno

E lentamente mi sento svenire

Mentre il ricordo
Fragile riflesso
Di nuovo prevale

Ricordo

DE SOLITVDINE

Your lips
Talk
About the emptiness that surrounds me

About solitude

Your kisses
Cast
The blue shadow of the moon
On my mouth
And my love itself
Interpenetrate

I am in your womb
The unborn beginning to die

We turned our eyes
On a *fading* world

I would like you to remain with me

About emptiness

LABRA TVA
DE SOLITVDINE ME CIRCVMDANTI
LOQVVNTVR

DE LONGINQVITATE

BASIA TVA
IN MEA ORE
CAERVLEAM LVNAE VMBRAM
IACTANT
ET MEVS IPSE AMOR
EA ME IMBVIT

IN GREMIO TVO
NON NATVS INCIPIENS MORI SVM

IN DISSOLVENTES TERRAS
OCVLOS CONVERTIMVS

VT MECVM MANERES VELLEREM

DE SOLITVDINE

Le tue labbra
Parlano
Del vuoto che mi circonda

Della lontananza

I tuoi baci
Proiettano
L'ombra blu della luna
Sulla mia bocca
Ed il mio amore stesso
Me ne compenetra

Sono entro il tuo grembo
Il non nato che inizia a morire

Abbiamo rivolto il nostro sguardo
Su un mondo *in dissoluzione*

Vorrei che rimanessi con me

Del vuoto

VERBIS VIRGO

Feminine spectres
Outline
Ocean
Like restless points

Reflections unravel

Violence
Explains
In demons
Exhausting human *dances*

And to me
Pours out in palms
A tannic wine
Of spices

Virgin of words
I find peace in mute lips

Virgin of words

FEMINEAE VMBRAE
MARE
DELINEANT
QVASI INQVIETA PVNCTA

REPERCVSSVS DIFFVNDVNTVR

VIS
IN DAEMONIBVS
DEBILITANTES HVMANAS CHOREAS
EXPLICAT

ET MIHI
IN PALMIS
ADSTRINGENS AROMATIS MERVM
INFVNDIT

VERBIS VIRGO
IN LABRIS MVTIS REQVIESCO

VERBIS VIRGO

Femminei spettri
Disegnano
Oceano
Quasi irrequieti punti

Dipanano riflessi

La violenza
Esplica
In demoni
Estenuanti *danze* umane

Ed a me
Versa in palmi
Un vino tànnico
Di spezie

Vergine di parole
Trovo riposo in labbra mute

Vergine di parole

TREMOR

Lovable Sappho
You come close with faint feet
You sweetly take my hand

You invite me to sit by you
On the brown soil
Far from these deafening noises

You come close
With moist lips
You whisper
Of the purple flowers
Of Lydia

Of the desire
Of fragrant hyacinths

With great effort I dissimulate
The tremble that shakes me

Unhealable

Tremble

AMABILIS SAPPHO
LEVIBVS PEDIBVS ADPROPINQVAS
DVLCE MANV ME COMPREHENDIS

VT APVD TE SEDEAM VOCAS
IN FVSCA TERRA
PROCVL AB HIS OBTVNDENTIBVS FRAGORIBVS

VDIS LABRIS
ADCEDIS
SVSVRRAS
DE PVRPVREIS FLORIBVS
LYDIIS

DE FRAGRANTIVM HYACINTHORVM
CVPIDITATE

VIX TREMOREM ME CONCVTIENTEM
DISSIMVLO

INSANABILEM

TREMOR

Amabile Saffo
Ti avvicini con piedi lievi
Mi prendi dolcemente per mano

Mi inviti a sederti accanto
Sulla terra bruna
Lontano da questi rumori assordanti

Ti avvicini
Con labbra umide
Mi sussurri
Dei fiori porpora
Di Lidia

Del desiderio
Di giacinti profumati

A fatica dissimulo
Il tremito che mi scuote

Insanabile

Tremito

TE EXSPECTABAM

I sleep alone
In the soft bed
Of white Attalic fabrics

An Ethiopian myrrh burns in the air
Whilst
I pour a scent
Of sweetest spices

I listen to the wind speaking of you

You finally came

I have been waiting for you

Waiting for you

DORMIO SOLA
IN MOLLI LECTO
CANDIDIS TEXTILIBVS ATTALICĪS

MYRRHA AETHIOPICA IN AERE ARDET
DVM
DVLCISSIMORVM ODOREM AROMATVM
EFFVNDO

AVSCVLTO VENTVM DE TE LOQVENTEM

TANDEM ADVENISTI

TE EXSPECTABAM

TE EXSPECTABAM

Dormo sola
Nel letto soffice
Di candide stoffe attaliche

Una mirra etiope brucia nell'aria
Mentre
Verso un profumo
Di spezie dolcissime

Ascolto il vento parlarmi di te

Sei finalmente giunta

Ti aspettavo

Ti aspettavo

ANIMA DVPLEX

On your face
Trembling
Pianoforte vibrations

In blue tears
Of ocean
Expose
Transparencies

In your eyes
Sudden reflection
Of twofold soul

Twofold soul

IN VVLTV TVO
TREMVLAE
NVTATIONES CLAVICHORDII

IN CAERVLEIS LACRIMIS
MARIS
PERLVCIDITATES
IMPRIMVNT

IN OCVLIS TVIS
SVBITVS REPERCVSSVS
DVPLICIS ANIMAE

ANIMA DVPLEX

Sul tuo volto
Tremule
Vibrazioni di pianoforte

In pianto blu
Di oceano
Impressionano
Trasparenze

Nei tuoi occhi
Subitaneo riflesso
Di anima duplice

Anima duplice

SEPTEMBER

September dissolves
In vain tears

Thou
Beloved vestal
Lie
Buried
Beneath blue silence

And the crying generates roses
For an unborn visage

Remembrance fades with me
As we lose

Forever

September

SEPTEMBER
IN INANIBVS LACHRIMIS DISSOLVITVR

TV
AMATA VESTALIS
IACES
IN CAERVLEIS SILENTIIS
HVMATA

AC FLETVS NON NATO VVLTVI ROSAS
GIGNIT

RECORDATIO MECVM INCLINAT
DVM NOS PERDIMVS

IN AETERNVM

SEPTEMBER

Settembre si dissolve
In lacrime vane

Tu
Amata vestale
Giaci
Sepolta
Tra silenzio blu

Ed il pianto genera rose
Per un volto non nato

Il ricordo declina con me
Mentre noi perdiamo

Per sempre

Settembre

MELILOTOS AVREA

These thorns in my side
Breed tears
Rough

Red of oxidised iron

Dried
By the warm wind of Syria

You can see their reflection in my eyes

Whilst I observe the sand of the African coast
Among the golden fields of melilot
To deposit at last

Golden melilot

HAE SPINAE IN LATERE MEO
LACRIMAS GIGNVNT
SCABRAS

FERRO ROBIGINE OBDVCTO RVBRAS

EXSICCATAS
CALIDO VENTO SYRIACO

EARVM REPERCVSSVM IN OCVLIS MEIS VIDERE POTES

DVM LITORVM AFRICANORVM ARENAM
IN AVREOS MELILOTIS AGROS
TANDEM SVBSIDERE INTVEOR

MELILOTOS AVREA

Queste spine nel mio fianco
Generano lacrime
Scabre

Rosse di ferro ossidato

Asciugate
Dal vento caldo di Siria

Puoi vederne il riflesso nei miei occhi

Mentre osservo la sabbia delle coste africane
Fra i campi dorati di meliloto
Finalmentre depositarsi

Meliloto dorato

ZACYNTHVS

The wind stopped
The light of the sunset sweetly vanishes

I remain alone in front of the sea of Zakynthos
I feel its caress on my skin
The gentle movement

Again myself

With no love
With no remorse

Almost a new son of Arcadia

I am finally able to remember

Zakynthos

VENTVS CONSIDIT
LVX OCCASVS LENITER EVANESCIT

SOLVS ANTE PONTI ZACYNTHII AEQVOR
EIVS TACTVM SVPER CVTIM MEAM SENTIO
LEVEM MOTVM

DENVO EGOMET

SINE AMORE
SINE ANIMI CONSCIENTIA

QVASI NOVVS ARCADIAE FILIVS

TANDEM MEMINISSE POSSVM

ZACYNTHVS

Il vento si è fermato
Svanisce dolcemente la luce del tramonto

Rimango solo di fronte al mare di Zacinto
Ne sento la carezza sulla mia pelle
Il movimento lieve

Di nuovo me stesso

Senza amore
Senza rimorso

Quasi un nuovo figlio di Arcadia

Finalmente riesco a ricordare

Zacinto

SEPVLCRVM ADLICIENS

Oppressive hours
Of a night beaten by the wind of insomnia
Amongst the naked vineyards
Contorted
In fields arid of silver

My limbs
Worn
Are reflected on your eyes
With the soft lashes

Your tumid lips
Desire
The memory of my body
Pallid

Inside your womb
Seducing tomb
Our remembrance is shapen by a pale light

Seducing tomb

HORAE GRAVES
INSOMNIARVM VENTO PERCVSSAE NOCTIS
NVDA INTER VINETA
DETORTA
ARGENTEIS IN ARIDIS AGRIS

MEMBRA MEA
CONSVMPTA
AD OCVLOS TVOS MOLLIBVS CILIIS
REDEVNT

TVMIDA LABRA TVA
MEMORIAM CORPORIS MEI
EXANGVIS
CVPIVNT

IN SINV TVO
SEPVLCRO ADLICIENTI
RECORDATIO NOSTRA PALLIDA LVCE FINGITVR

SEPVLCRVM ADLICIENS

Ore pesanti
Di una notte percossa dal vento d'insonnia
Fra i vigneti nudi
Contorti
In campi aridi d'argento

Le mie membra
Logore
Si riflettono sui tuoi occhi
Dalle ciglia morbide

Le tue labbra tumide
Desiderano
La memoria del mio corpo
Esangue

Entro il tuo seno
Tomba seducente
Il nostro ricordo si finge di pallida luce

Tomba seducente

SMYRNA

Lydia
The first days of autumn

Faint flutes reverberate far
Whilst slowly we walk
Under the sun of Smyrna

Then we stop
In unreal silence

Now alone
I taste perpetual instants
Only beaten by the wind

Under the smoldering sun
Sweat frames my features
Runs along my eyelids
Burns eyes blinded
By the intense light of noon

I feel on my hands the sand
The physicity of the moment
Blocking my breath

I briefly observe
The wind caressing the hair of my beloved
Standing to my side

Since all times I have been waiting for this moment
My lover
Since all times

I have never been so ready

Smyrna

LYDIA
PRIMIS AVTVMNI DIEBVS

TENVES TIBIAE EX LONGINQVO RESONANT
DVM LENTE SOLIBVS SMYRNAE EXPOSITI
PROCEDIMVS

CONSISTIMVS POSTEA
VANO SILENTIO

NVNC SOLVS
GVSTO INTERMINATA TEMPORIS MOMENTA
SOLVM VENTO SIGNATA

FERVIDIS SOLIBVS EXPOSITVS
SVDOR LINEAMENTA CIRCVMDAT
SECVNDVM PALPEBRAS FLVIT
PENETRAT OCVLOS PRAESTRICTOS
VEHEMENTI MERIDIEI LVCE

ARENAM IN MANIBVS MEIS SENTIO
MOMENTI PERSPICVITATEM
SPIRITVM INTERCLVDERE

BREVITER INTVEOR
VENTVM PERMVLCERE CAPILLVM AMATI
MIHI VICINI

PERPETVO HOC MOMENTVM EXSPECTO
AMANS MEVS
PERPETVO

NVMQVAM TAM PARATVS FVI

SMYRNA

Lidia
I primi giorni dell'autunno

Tenui flauti risuonano lontano
Mentre camminiamo lentamente
Sotto il sole di Smirne

Poi ci fermiamo
In silenzio irreale

Ora solo
Assaporo attimi interminabili
Unicamente scanditi dal vento

Sotto il sole rovente
Il sudore incornicia i lineamenti
Scorre lungo le palpebre
Penetra occhi accecati
Dalla luce intensa del meriggio

Avverto sulle mie mani la sabbia
La fisicità del momento
Bloccare il respiro

Guardo brevemente
Il vento accarezzare i capelli dell'amato
A me vicino

Da sempre attendo questo momento
Mio amante
Da sempre

Non sono mai stato così pronto

Smirne

CRVCI AFFIXVS

Take my corrupted femininity
My youth of ephebos

A dark rain
Desecrating
Draws with oxidized copper
The skin
Around the hips

Descends within the groin
Coagulates its heavy residue

Livid
Of three hundred days
Of rage

Corrupted femininity

CAPE CORRVPTAM VIM MEAM MVLIEBREM
ADVLESCENTIAM MEAM EPHEBI

OBSCVRVS IMBER
BLASPHEMVS
AERE ROBIGINE OBDVCTO
DELINEAT CVTIM
CIRCVM LATERA

INTRA INGVINA DESCENDIT
COAGVLAT GRAVE RESIDVVM SVVM

LIVIDVVM
TRECENTIS DIEBVS
IRAE

CRVCI AFFIXVS

Prendi la mia femminilità corrotta
La mia giovinezza di efebo

Una pioggia scura
Dissacrante
Disegna di rame ossidato
La pelle
Attorno ai fianchi

Scende entro l'inguine
Coagula il suo residuo pesante

Livido
Di trecento giorni
Di rabbia

Femminilità corrotta

INTACTAE FRAGRANTIAE

The green of my eyes
Contemplates
Virgin fragrances

Whilst
Remote scents of orange
Most bitter

Lightly touch the sea of salt
Under the silent cliffs
Of Leukas

Virgin fragrances

OCVLI MEI VIRIDES
INTACTAS FRAGRANTIAS
INTVENTVR

DVM
REMOTI MEDICAE ARBORIS ODORES
AMARISSIMI

LEVITER SALSVM PONTVM ADTINGVNT
SILENTIBVS SVB SCOPVLIS
LEVCADIS

INTACTAE FRAGRANTIAE

Il verde dei miei occhi
Contempla
Fragranze vergini

Mentre
Remoti profumi d'arancio
Amarissimi

Sfiorano il mare salato
Sotto le silenziose scogliere
Di Leukas

Fragranze vergini

IN IMAGINIBVS

Illuminates me
The shadow of the woman who followed me

My eyes
Blinded by reflections
Observe
In frames
The wandering of the light robe

The bare back
The thin wrists

A scent
Of urban pollen
Recomposes
The film of time

In frames

ME INLVMINAT
VMBRA MVLIERIS QVAE ME SEQVEBATVR

OCVLI MEI
REPERCVSSIBVS PRAESTRICTI
OBSERVANT
IN EXPRESSIS LVCE IMAGINIBVS
LEVEM VESTEM VOLITANTEM

DORSVM NVDVM
SVBTILES MANVS

SVAVIS ODOR
VRBANI POLLINIS
PELLICVLAM TEMPORIS
COMPONIT

IN IMAGINIBVS

Mi illumina
L'ombra della donna che mi seguiva

I miei occhi
Accecati di riflessi
Osservano
In fotogrammi
Il vagare della veste leggera

La schiena nuda
I polsi sottili

Un profumo
Di polline urbano
Ricompone
La pellicola del tempo

In fotogrammi

AMO

I love your hair of violet
Your purest face
Your skin
Illuminated by the faint fingers of the moon

I adore your lovable smile
Whilst you tell me
Of the pleasures of your exquisite existence

The lyricism of your verse
Moves in me
A sentiment with no reservations

Unrestrainable

I love

AMO CAPILLVM TVVM VIOLAE
TVVM VVLTVM PVRISSIMVM
CVTIM TVAM
TENVIBVS LVNAE DIGITIS INLVMINATAM

DILIGO AMABILEM RISVM TVVM
DVM NARRAS
DE MOLLITIIS EXQVISITAE VITAE TVAE

LYRICVS VERSVVM TVORVM FERVOR
ANIMVM SINE EXCEPTIONE
IN ME MOVET

EFFRENATVM

AMO

Amo i tuoi capelli di viola
Il tuo volto purissimo
La tua pelle
Illuminata dalle tenui dita della Luna

Adoro il tuo amabile sorriso
Mentre mi racconti
Delle dolcezze della tua esistenza squisita

La liricità del tuo verso
Muove in me
Un sentimento senza riserve

Irrefrenabile

Amo

VIRIDIS ETRVSCVM

The desert of waters
Parts the morning brume

Turbid water
Of immobile Etruscan green

Reflects arid rocks livid of ash
Celebrates the inevitable release
Of existence

The breath of the sun stops at the entrance of the port

And the Florentine cypresses pressed in the shade
Interpenetrate the air with fragrance of absence

Amongst the filigree of the hair
The eyes search their way

Catch sight of the white tunic
Flowing

And receive a cold embrace
Human
Free

Whilst the fog lifts
In interminable silences

In perpetuum soror
Ave atqve vale

Etruscan green

SOLITVDO AQVARVM
MANE BRVMAS RECLVDIT

OBSCVRA AQVA
ETRVSCO EX IMMOTO VIRIDI

ARIDAS RVPES EX CINERE LIVIDAS REPERCVTIT
CELEBRAT INEVITABILEM RELICTIONEM
VITAE

AVRA SOLIS IN ORE PORTVS CONSISTIT

ET FLORENTINAE CVPRESSVS IN VMBRA DENSETAE
AEREM EX ODORE ABSENTIAE PERMEANT

INTER FILORVM GRANVM CAPILLI
OCVLI ADITVM SCRVTANTVR

ASPICIVNT CANDIDAM TVNICAM
PROMISSAM

ET AB EA FRIGIDVM AMPLEXVM ACCIPIVNT
HVMANVM
LIBERVM

DVM CALIGO DISCVTITVR
DIVTINIS SILENTIIS

*IN PERPETVVM SOROR
AVE ATQVE VALE*

VIRIDIS ETRVSCVM

Il deserto delle acque
Schiude le brume del mattino

Acqua scura
Di immobile verde etrusco

Riflette aride rocce livide di cenere
Celebra il rilascio inevitabile
Dell'esistenza

L'alito del sole si ferma ai margini del porto

Ed i cipressi fiorentini stretti in ombra
Permeano l'aria d'aroma d'assenza

Fra la filigrana dei capelli
Gli occhi cercano un varco

Scorgono la bianca tunica
Fluente

E ne ricevono un abbraccio freddo
Umano
Libero

Mentre la nebbia si solleva
In interminabili silenzi

In perpetvvm soror
Ave atqve vale

Verde etrusco

MEL

A waft of funereal honey
Adorns
Your lips of pearls

Honey

FVNEBRI EX MELLE EFFLVVIVM
ORNAT
LABRVM TVVM MARGARITIS

MEL

Effluvio di miele funereo
Adorna
Il tuo labbro imperlato

Miele

AMYGDALVS

Fellow disciple of the soul
The almond of your garden
In me flowers again

Almond

ANIMAE CONDISCIPVLVS
HORTI TVI AMYGDALVS
IN ME REFLORESCIT

AMYGDALVS

Condiscepolo dell'anima
Il mandorlo del tuo giardino
In me rifiorisce

Mandorlo

TREPIDATIO

The pure skin of your slender ankles
Shakes me
Instintively I tremble

Tremble

CANDIDA CVTIS AGILIVM TALORVM TVORVM
ME COMMOVET
SPONTE TREPIDO

TREPIDATIO

La pelle candida delle tue snelle caviglie
Mi scuote
Istintivamente fremo

Fremore

VVLTVS

Faces empty of names
Spread *hate*
Within the shadow of glances

Vvltvs

VVLTVS A NOMINIBVS VACVI
OCVLORVM INTRA VMBRAM
ODIVM DISSEMINANT

VVLTVS

VVLTVS (detail)
Bronze and Cast Glass (17"x12"x12" · 43x30x30cm)

VVLTVS (detail)
Bronze and Cast Glass (17"x12"x12" · 43x30x30cm)

Volti vuoti di nomi
Disseminano *odio*
Entro l'ombra degli sguardi

Vvltvs

CYCLVS DIEI

I · FEMINEA AVRORA

I

A silent breath veiled of white
Slowly unravels gauzes
Of pale woven linen

Opens to the gentle awakening from the frost of onyx

On milky mists
Iridiscent

Hellenic almond trees
Reflect the silver waters of the estuary

Opalescent of thin violet haze

Empty words

A diffused beauty

Twofold light mutates colour
In the wrath of *day*

Feminine dawn

I

TACITA AVRA ALBO VELATA
LENITER LIGAMENTA EXPLICAT
EX CANDIDO LINO INTEXTO

INITIVM TENVI REDITVI AB GELO EX ONYCHE FACIT

SVPER LACTEAS CALIGINES
VARIAS

AMYGDALI GRAECI
ARGENTEAM ORIS AQVAM REMITTVNT

VIOLACEA NEBVLA SVBTILI ORNATI

VACVA VERBA

PVLCHRITVDO DIFFVSA

DVPLEX LVMEN COLOREM MVTAT
IN IRA *DIEI*

FEMINEA AVRORA

I

Un alito silente velato di bianco
Districa lentamente le garze
Di candido lino attorto

Apre al tenue risveglio dal gelo di onice

Su lattiginose brume
Iridescenti

Mandorli ellenici
Riflettono l'acqua argentea dell'estuario

Imperlato di viola nebbia sottile

Vacue parole

Una bellezza diffusa

Duplice chiarore trascolora
Nell'ira del *giorno*

Aurora femminea

CYCLVS DIEI

II · IRA DIEI

II

Friable light
Radiates on the humid cobbles of the luminous city

A sudden trepidation

Vehement

My dark skin
Parched
Breathes in a new poetry
Energetic
Golden

Noble

My body in uncontrollable movement
Inebriates of new senses
Of disorder
Of excess

Of first violation

The day darkens of arid hate

The burnt soil pales
In the *twilight* of sycamores

Wrath of day

228

II

LVX FRIABILIS
SVBITAM TREPIDATIONEM

VIOLENTAM

EXPOLITAE VRBIS IN VDA VIA SILICEA ILLVSTRAT

CVTIS MEA NIGRANS
ARIDA
IN NOVA POESE RESPIRAT
ACRI
AVREA

NOBILI

CORPVS MEVM IN VEHEMENTI MOTV
NOVIS SENSIBVS INEBRIAT
IMMODESTIA
INTEMPERANTIA

VIOLATIONE PRIMA

DIES ARIDO ODIO OBSCVRATVR

IN *CREPVSCVLO* SYCOMORORVM
VSTA TERRA LIVESCIT

IRA DIEI

II

Luce friabile
Irradia sul selciato umido della città lucida

Una trepidazione subitanea

Veemente

La mia pelle cupa
Riarsa
Respira in una poesia nuova
Energica
Aurea

Nobile

Il mio corpo in movimento convulso
Si inebria di nuovi sensi
Di disordine
D'eccesso

Di violazione prima

Il giorno si oscura di arido odio

La terra bruciata illividisce
Nel *crepuscolo* dei sicomori

Ira del giorno

CYCLVS DIEI

III · CREPVSCVLVM SYCOMORORVM

III

Acrid twilights
Reveal mute gardens never accessed

Harmonic architecture
Projects a circle of shadow
Humid and transparent

The council of poets

Beneath the glaucus olive tree of the ionic modulations

A tacit presence
Nourishes me with virginal trembling

Lids reveal the umid eyes
Of the internal monologue

Light quiets
In *night* of Lethe

Twilight of sycamores

III

ACRIA CREPVSCVLA
MVTOS HORTOS INACCESSOS DETEGVNT

CONSONA ARCHITECTVRA
CIRCVLVM VMBRAE INCLINAT
PERLVCIDAE ET VDAE

CONCILIVM POETARVM

SVB GLAVCA OLIVA IONICIS MODVLATIONIBVS

PRAESENTIA TACITA
ME TREMORE VIRGINALI ALIT

PALPEBRAE VDOS INTIMI SERMONIS OCVLOS
RECLVDVNT

LVX TACET
IN *NOCTE* LETHAEA

CREPVSCVLVM SYCOMORORVM

III

Acri crepuscoli
Dischiudono muti giardini inaccessi

Architettura armonica
Declina un cerchio d'ombra
Umida e trasparente

Il concilio dei poeti

Sotto il glauco olivo dalle modulazioni ioniche

Una tacita presenza
Mi nutre di tremito verginale

Le palpebre schiudono gli occhi umidi
Del monologo interiore

Si tace la luce
In *notte* letea

Crepuscolo dei sicomori

CYCLVS DIEI

IV · NOX LETHAEA

IV

Necropolis
Cloudy shadow hidden amongst the bitterness of the port

Caressed by livid silent light

The marble

Glass of opal
Breathes poetry in lifeless air

Reclined the visage
Veiled with linen
With no words
I await the inevitable release

The quiet decline of the gentle warmth

My body unburied
Stripped of any belonging
Finally glabrous

Inebriates of exquisite melancholies

And my eyes mute of ashes
The eyelids motionless

Tremble of words

In feminine *dawn*

Night of Lethe

IV

SEPVLCRETVM
TVRBIDA VMBRA PORTVS IN AMARITVDINE ABDITA

LIVIDA LVCE TACITA PERMVLCTA

MARMOR

EX OPALO VITRVM
POESIN IN INERTEM AEREM EXHALAT

RECLINATO VVLTV
LINO VELATO
SINE VERBO
INEVITABILEM RELICTIONEM EXSPECTO

LENTVM MITIS TEPORIS DECLIVE

CORPVS MEVM INSEPVLTVM
OMNI AMORE NVDATVM
AD VLTIMVM GLABRVM

INEBRIAT SVAVIBVS MAESTITIIS

ET OCVLI MEI EX CINERE MVTI
PALPEBRIS IMMOTIS

VERBIS TREPIDANT

IN FEMINEA *AVRORA*

NOX LETHAEA

IV

Necropoli
Torbida ombra nascosta fra l'amaro del porto

Accarezzata da livida luce tacita

Il marmo

Vetro di opale
Esala poesia in aria inerte

Reclinato il volto
Velato di lino
Senza parola
Aspetto il rilascio inevitabile

Il lento declivio del mite tepore

Il mio corpo insepolto
Spogliato da ogni appartenenza
Finalmente glabro

Si inebria di squisite malinconie

Ed i miei occhi muti di cenere
Le palpebre immote

Fremono di parole

In *aurora* femminea

Notte letea

"EGO TRANQVILLITATEM VOCO"

www.ingramcontent.com/pod-product-compliance
Lightning Source LLC
Chambersburg PA
CBHW030415100426
42812CB00028B/2974/J